Operation Paperclip: The Covert U.S. Program to Recruit German Nazi Scientists

Copyright Page

TITLE: Operation Paperclip: The Covert U.S. Program to Recruit German Nazi Scientists

1ST Edition

ISBN: 9798215894729

Table of Contents

Operation Paperclip: The Covert U.S. Program to Recruit German Nazi Scientists

By Roberto Miguel Rodriguez

Chapter 1: Operation Paperclip: The Covert U.S. Program to Recruit German Nazi Scientists

The Origins of Operation Paperclip

Operation Paperclip, an enigmatic and highly controversial covert program, played a pivotal role in shaping various aspects of our modern world. Its origins can be traced back to the final stages of World War II, when the United States found itself in a precarious position. The war had devastated Europe, leaving a trail of destruction and millions of lives lost. Amidst the ruins, however, lay a treasure trove of scientific knowledge and technological advancements that both the United States and the Soviet Union sought to claim for themselves.

In this subchapter, we delve into the origins of Operation Paperclip, exploring the factors that led to its inception and its subsequent impact on numerous fields.

As the war drew to a close, the United States, recognizing the value of German scientific expertise, initiated Operation Paperclip. Under this covert program, American intelligence agencies clandestinely recruited German Nazi scientists and engineers, offering them immunity from prosecution for war crimes in exchange for their knowledge and services. The primary objective was to prevent these brilliant minds from falling into the hands of the Soviet Union, who also sought to exploit their expertise.

The program's origins can be traced back to the realization that the potential advancements in technology and scientific knowledge possessed by the German scientists could provide a significant advantage in the emerging Cold War. The United States sought to harness the talents of these scientists to bolster its own military capabilities, particularly in the fields of rocketry, aeronautics, and nuclear research.

However, the decision to recruit former Nazi scientists sparked intense ethical controversies and moral dilemmas. Critics argued that by providing immunity to these individuals, the United States was effectively absolving them of their crimes and undermining the principles of justice. This aspect of Operation Paperclip continues to be a topic of debate among historians and scholars to this day.

Furthermore, Operation Paperclip left an indelible mark on various domains. The influence of these German scientists can be seen in the advancements made in space exploration, with their work contributing to the development of the Saturn V rocket and the eventual moon landing. Additionally, their expertise played a crucial role in shaping Cold War technology, intelligence and espionage operations, and even medical advancements.

In conclusion, the origins of Operation Paperclip lie in the immediate aftermath of World War II, as the United States sought to secure the scientific knowledge and expertise of German Nazi scientists. While the program's impact on various fields cannot be denied, the ethical controversies surrounding its inception continue to generate intense debates among historians and scholars.

The Justification for Recruiting Nazi Scientists

In the aftermath of World War II, Operation Paperclip emerged as a covert U.S. program aimed at recruiting German Nazi scientists. This subchapter explores the justifications behind this controversial initiative, shedding light on the motivations and the impact it had on various fields of research and development.

Operation Paperclip: The Covert U.S. Program to Recruit German Nazi Scientists sought to harness the scientific knowledge and expertise possessed by these individuals, despite their involvement in the atrocities committed under Nazi rule. Historians have debated the ethical controversies and moral dilemmas associated with this program, but understanding the justifications behind it is essential to grasp its significance.

One of the primary justifications for recruiting Nazi scientists was the urgent need to gain an edge in the emerging Cold War. The Soviet Union posed a significant threat to the United States, and the U.S. government believed that by recruiting these scientists, they could prevent them from falling into Soviet hands. This program played a crucial role in the development of space exploration, aeronautics, nuclear research, and intelligence operations, all critical areas during the Cold War.

Operation Paperclip had a profound impact on space exploration. German rocket scientists, led by Wernher von Braun, played a vital role in the development of the American space program. Their expertise paved the way for significant advancements, including the launch of the first American satellite and the eventual landing of humans on the moon.

Furthermore, the program's influence on Cold War technology cannot be overlooked. The recruitment of German scientists directly contributed to advancements in missile technology, nuclear research, and intelligence gathering. These scientists brought invaluable knowledge and experience that propelled the United States to the forefront of military and technological superiority during the Cold War.

Operation Paperclip also had a hidden contribution to medical advancements. Nazi scientists possessed expertise in various medical fields, including immunology, neurology, and genetics. Their knowledge and research findings were utilized in post-war medical research, leading to significant breakthroughs in areas such as organ transplantation, vaccine development, and understanding the human brain.

Despite its undeniable contributions, Operation Paperclip remains shrouded in ethical controversies. The decision to recruit scientists involved in war crimes raised questions of moral responsibility. Critics argue that by allowing these individuals to escape prosecution, the U.S. compromised its own principles. The legacy of Operation Paperclip raises challenging questions about the balance between scientific progress and moral accountability.

In conclusion, the justifications for recruiting Nazi scientists under Operation Paperclip were primarily rooted in geopolitical concerns and the need to gain an advantage in the Cold War. The program's impact on space exploration, Cold War technology, medical advancements, intelligence operations, and various other fields cannot be understated. However, the ethical controversies and moral dilemmas surrounding this initiative continue to provoke debate among historians and researchers to this day. Understanding the nuances of this chapter in history is crucial to assessing its lasting legacy.

The Recruitment Process and Selection Criteria

In the subchapter titled "The Recruitment Process and Selection Criteria," we delve into the intricate details of Operation Paperclip, the covert U.S. program that recruited German Nazi scientists. This chapter aims to provide historians and enthusiasts with a comprehensive understanding of how the recruitment process unfolded and the selection criteria employed.

Operation Paperclip, initiated in the aftermath of World War II, aimed to harness the scientific knowledge and expertise of German scientists for the benefit of the United States. The recruitment process was meticulously planned and executed by U.S. intelligence agencies, with the goal of identifying the most qualified and valuable scientists.

The selection criteria for Operation Paperclip were multifaceted, focusing on scientific proficiency, expertise, and potential contributions to various fields. Scientists with expertise in a wide range of disciplines, including aerospace engineering, medicine, intelligence, nuclear research, and chemical warfare, were sought after.

The recruitment process primarily targeted scientists who had not been directly involved in war crimes or crimes against humanity. However, the criteria were not without controversy, as some individuals with questionable pasts were still included in the program. The chapter explores the ethical controversies and moral dilemmas surrounding Operation Paperclip's selection process, shedding light on the difficult decisions made by U.S. authorities.

Furthermore, this subchapter examines the impact of Operation Paperclip on various niches, such as space exploration, Cold War technology, the arms race, medical advancements, intelligence, espionage, aeronautics, nuclear research, chemical warfare, cybersecurity, and cryptography. By analyzing the influence of German Nazi scientists in these fields, historians can gain a nuanced perspective on the lasting legacy of Operation Paperclip.

Through this subchapter, historians can gain valuable insights into the recruitment process and selection criteria employed by Operation Paperclip. By exploring the ethical controversies, moral dilemmas, and the far-reaching impact of the program, a more comprehensive understanding of this covert U.S. operation can be achieved.

Controversial Figures: Werner Von Braun and Arthur Rudolph

In the annals of history, few figures evoke as much controversy as Werner Von Braun and Arthur Rudolph. These two German scientists played significant roles in the U.S. program known as Operation Paperclip, which aimed to recruit German Nazi scientists following World War

II. Their contributions to various fields, particularly space exploration and technology, are undeniable, but their past affiliations with the Nazi regime have raised ethical controversies and moral dilemmas that continue to be debated today.

Werner Von Braun, often hailed as the father of modern rocketry, was a pivotal figure in the development of the V-2 rocket during the war. Under his leadership, the V-2 became a devastating weapon, causing immense destruction in London and other European cities. Despite his involvement in the Nazi war machine, Von Braun was recruited by the United States, and his expertise was instrumental in launching America's space program. He played a key role in the development of the Saturn V rocket, which successfully carried astronauts to the moon during the Apollo missions.

Similarly, Arthur Rudolph, an accomplished engineer, was responsible for the design and production of the V-2 rocket. His expertise in rocketry made him a valuable asset to the United States, and he played a crucial role in the development of the Saturn V. However, Rudolph's past involvement in the use of forced labor during the war raised ethical concerns. He was later stripped of his U.S. citizenship and returned to Germany, where he faced charges related to his war crimes.

The inclusion of Von Braun and Rudolph in Operation Paperclip has had a profound impact on various fields. Their contributions to space exploration and technology were undeniable, shaping the course of human history. However, their involvement with the Nazi regime raises questions about the ethical implications of their recruitment by the United States. Should the United States have turned a blind eye to their past actions in exchange for their scientific knowledge and expertise?

This subchapter delves into the controversial figures of Werner Von Braun and Arthur Rudolph, examining their contributions to Operation Paperclip and their subsequent impact on space exploration, technology, and other fields. By exploring the ethical controversies and moral dilemmas surrounding their involvement, historians can gain a deeper understanding of the complex legacy of Operation Paperclip and its hidden influence on various aspects of society, from aeronautics to intelligence and espionage.

The Integration of German Scientists into the U.S. Scientific Community

The integration of German scientists into the U.S. scientific community after World War II is a fascinating and significant chapter in the history of science and technology. Operation Paperclip, the covert U.S. program that recruited German Nazi scientists, played a crucial role in shaping various fields, from space exploration to medical advancements and intelligence.

Following the end of World War II, the United States sought to gain an edge in the emerging Cold War with the Soviet Union. Recognizing the scientific achievements of German scientists, particularly in rocketry and aerospace technology, the U.S. government embarked on a secret mission to recruit them. Operation Paperclip aimed to harness the knowledge and expertise of these scientists for the benefit of American interests.

The impact of Operation Paperclip on space exploration cannot be overstated. German scientists, led by Wernher von Braun, were instrumental in the development of America's space program. Their expertise in rocketry propelled the U.S. to achieve significant milestones, including the successful launch of the Explorer 1 satellite and the Apollo moon missions.

Moreover, Operation Paperclip had a profound influence on Cold War technology. German scientists contributed to the development of advanced weaponry, such as the intercontinental ballistic missile, which played a pivotal role in maintaining the balance of power during the arms race. Their involvement in intelligence and espionage also helped the United States gain valuable insight into Soviet activities.

However, the program was not without its controversies and moral dilemmas. Many of the German scientists recruited under Operation Paperclip had affiliations with the Nazi regime and were involved in war crimes. The ethical implications of welcoming these scientists into the U.S. scientific community sparked debates among historians and the public alike.

Operation Paperclip also left an enduring legacy in various other fields. German scientists played a significant role in advancing aeronautics, nuclear research, and chemical warfare. Additionally, their undisclosed impact on cybersecurity and cryptography remains a topic of interest and speculation.

In conclusion, the integration of German scientists into the U.S. scientific community through Operation Paperclip had far-reaching consequences. From space exploration to intelligence gathering, their contributions shaped the course of history. However, the program's ethical controversies and moral dilemmas continue to generate debate among historians and researchers. Understanding this chapter in history is crucial for comprehending the complex interplay between scientific progress, politics, and ethics.

Chapter 2: Operation Paperclip: The Impact on Space Exploration

The Role of German Scientists in the Development of V-2 Rockets

Title: The Role of German Scientists in the Development of V-2 Rockets

Introduction:

In the subchapter "The Role of German Scientists in the Development of V-2 Rockets," we delve into the significant contributions made by German scientists as part of Operation Paperclip, the covert U.S. program to recruit German Nazi scientists. This section explores the impact of these scientists on the development of V-2 rocket technology, a pivotal advancement in aerospace engineering with far-reaching consequences.

Content:

The V-2 rocket, developed during World War II, stands as a testament to the immense knowledge and expertise possessed by German scientists. Operation Paperclip played a crucial role in transferring this expertise to the United States. Under the program, talented scientists, including Wernher von Braun, were recruited to work on rocket technology in the U.S.

The German scientists brought with them a wealth of knowledge acquired during their time in Nazi Germany. They had already made significant progress in developing the V-2 rocket, a groundbreaking achievement that pushed the boundaries of rocketry. This expertise, combined with the resources and infrastructure available in the U.S., allowed for even greater advancements.

The V-2 rocket represented a leap forward in rocket technology, becoming the world's first long-range guided ballistic missile. It was a devastating weapon, capable of striking targets hundreds of miles away with unparalleled accuracy. The German scientists' expertise in propulsion, guidance systems, and aerodynamics played a pivotal role in its development.

Furthermore, the V-2 program had a lasting impact beyond the war. The knowledge gained from developing the V-2 rocket formed the foundation for future advancements in space exploration. The German scientists, now working under U.S. leadership, continued to push the boundaries of rocket technology, eventually leading to the establishment of NASA and the successful Apollo moon missions.

Conclusion:

The contributions of German scientists through Operation Paperclip in the development of V-2 rockets cannot be understated. Their expertise propelled the United States to the forefront of rocket technology, laying the groundwork for future advancements in space exploration and shaping the course of history. The V-2 program not only showcased the immense talent of these scientists but also highlighted the complex ethical controversies and moral dilemmas surrounding Operation Paperclip. Understanding their role in the development of V-2 rockets allows us to recognize the hidden contributions made by these German scientists in various fields, from aeronautics to intelligence, espionage, medical advancements, and even cryptography.

Operation Paperclip's Influence on the U.S. Space Program

Operation Paperclip, the covert U.S. program that recruited German Nazi scientists, had a profound influence on the U.S. space program. This subchapter will delve into the various ways in which Operation Paperclip shaped and advanced space exploration.

One of the key contributions of the German scientists brought to the United States under Operation Paperclip was their expertise in rocketry. Led by Wernher von Braun, a visionary engineer and former member of the Nazi Party, these scientists played a pivotal role in the development of the American space program. Their knowledge and experience with the V-2 rocket, which they had developed for the Nazis during World War II, laid the foundation for the creation of the Redstone rocket, the first American ballistic missile. This breakthrough in rocket technology paved the way for the subsequent development of the Saturn V, the rocket that propelled the Apollo missions to the moon.

Additionally, Operation Paperclip scientists contributed to the advancement of guidance systems and navigation technology. They brought with them invaluable expertise in developing innovative guidance systems, such as gyroscopes and accelerometers, which were crucial for the successful launch and trajectory of space vehicles. These advancements not only improved the accuracy of rocket launches but also played a vital role in space exploration by enabling precise navigation and course corrections.

Moreover, the German scientists' expertise in materials science greatly influenced the U.S. space program. They introduced new materials and manufacturing techniques that enhanced the performance and durability of spacecraft. For instance, their knowledge of high-strength alloys and composite materials helped improve the design and construction of space capsules and satellite components, making them more resistant to extreme temperatures and providing better protection for astronauts.

Beyond their technical contributions, Operation Paperclip scientists played a crucial role in shaping the organizational and operational aspects of the U.S. space program. Their experience in managing large-scale scientific projects, combined with their rigorous work ethic, helped establish efficient research and development practices. They instilled a culture of discipline, precision, and relentless pursuit of excellence that became the hallmark of the American space program.

In conclusion, Operation Paperclip had a profound influence on the U.S. space program. By bringing in German scientists with their expertise in rocketry, guidance systems, materials science, and organizational practices, the program propelled the American space program to new heights. The legacy of these scientists can be seen in the successful moon landings, the development of advanced spacecraft, and the ongoing exploration of the cosmos. Their contributions continue to shape the field of space exploration and inspire future generations of scientists and engineers.

The Contributions of German Scientists to NASA

When it comes to the field of space exploration, the contributions made by German scientists recruited under Operation Paperclip cannot be overstated. These brilliant minds, who were once affiliated with the Nazi regime, played a crucial role in shaping NASA and its endeavors.

Under the covert U.S. program, Operation Paperclip, which aimed to harness the scientific expertise of former German Nazi scientists, many German scientists found themselves working for NASA. Their knowledge and expertise were instrumental in propelling the United States to the forefront of space exploration during the Cold War era.

One of the most notable contributions of these scientists was their involvement in the development of the V-2 rocket. Led by Wernher von Braun, a former member of the Nazi Party and the SS, the German scientists leveraged their expertise in rocketry to develop advanced propulsion systems that would later become the backbone of NASA's space program. The V-2 rocket, initially built as a weapon of war, served as a precursor to the Saturn V rocket, which successfully launched the Apollo missions and put the first man on the moon.

Furthermore, German scientists played a crucial role in advancing aeronautics and astronautics. Their expertise in aerodynamics and aircraft design led to significant advancements in spacecraft technology, allowing for safer and more efficient space travel. Their contributions laid the foundation for future space missions and paved the way for the development of the Space Shuttle program.

In addition to their impact on space exploration, German scientists recruited under Operation Paperclip also made significant contributions to other fields. Their expertise in intelligence and espionage was utilized by the U.S. government, aiding in Cold War era intelligence operations. Their involvement in nuclear research and chemical warfare, although controversial, provided valuable insights into these areas, which had far-reaching implications for national security and technological advancements.

However, it is important to acknowledge the ethical controversies and moral dilemmas surrounding Operation Paperclip. The decision to recruit former Nazi scientists was met with criticism, as their involvement in war crimes and human rights abuses cast a shadow over their contributions. The legacy of Operation Paperclip remains a subject of debate among historians, highlighting the complexity of balancing scientific advancements with ethical considerations.

Nevertheless, the contributions of German scientists recruited under Operation Paperclip cannot be ignored. Their expertise and knowledge played a pivotal role in shaping NASA's achievements, pushing the boundaries of space exploration, and leaving a lasting impact on fields such as aeronautics, intelligence, and nuclear research. Their work laid the foundation for future generations of scientists and engineers, shaping the trajectory of space exploration and scientific advancements for years to come.

The Legacy of Operation Paperclip in Space Exploration

Operation Paperclip, the covert U.S. program that recruited German Nazi scientists, left an indelible mark on various fields, including space exploration. This subchapter delves into the significant legacy of Operation Paperclip in shaping the trajectory of space exploration and the advancements made by the German scientists who were brought to America.

After World War II, the United States' desire to gain an edge in the Cold War prompted the recruitment of German scientists, many of whom had expertise in rocketry and aeronautics. Wernher von Braun, the renowned German engineer, was one such scientist who played a pivotal role in Operation Paperclip. His expertise in rocket technology proved invaluable to the United States, as he contributed to the development of the Redstone and Jupiter-C rockets, which were critical in launching America's first satellite, Explorer 1, in 1958.

The legacy of Operation Paperclip in space exploration extends beyond rocketry. The German scientists brought with them a wealth of knowledge and experience in various scientific disciplines. They played a crucial role in the establishment of NASA in 1958, and their expertise propelled the United States to become a global leader in space exploration.

Under von Braun's leadership, the German scientists contributed to the Apollo program, which ultimately led to the first manned moon landing in 1969. Their expertise in propulsion systems and guidance technology was instrumental in the success of this historic achievement.

Furthermore, the German scientists' influence on space exploration extended to the development of space shuttles. Their expertise in aerodynamics, materials science, and engineering significantly contributed to the creation of the Space Shuttle program, allowing for reusable spacecraft and revolutionizing the way humans explore space.

However, the legacy of Operation Paperclip in space exploration also raises ethical controversies and moral dilemmas. The recruitment of former Nazi scientists, who had been complicit in war crimes, poses questions about the United States' priorities and the extent to which scientific advancements should outweigh ethical considerations.

Despite these controversies, there is no denying the lasting impact of Operation Paperclip on space exploration. The German scientists brought with them a wealth of knowledge and expertise that propelled the United States to the forefront of space exploration. Their contributions continue to shape the field, serving as a testament to the complex legacy of Operation Paperclip in the pursuit of scientific advancements.

Chapter 3: Operation Paperclip: The Influence on Cold War Technology

The Transfer of German Technological Expertise to the U.S.

Operation Paperclip: Unveiling the Covert U.S. Program that Recruited German Nazi Scientists

The transfer of German technological expertise to the U.S. during and after World War II was a crucial aspect of Operation Paperclip, a covert U.S. program that recruited German Nazi scientists. This subchapter explores the impact of this transfer on various fields, including space exploration, cold war technology, arms race, medical advancements, intelligence and espionage, aeronautics, nuclear research, chemical warfare, cybersecurity, and cryptography.

Operation Paperclip played a significant role in shaping the trajectory of space exploration. German scientists such as Wernher von Braun, who were instrumental in developing the V-2 rocket during the war, brought their expertise to the U.S. They became key figures in the development of the American space program, including the establishment of NASA and the Apollo missions to the moon.

In the context of the Cold War, Operation Paperclip bolstered American technological capabilities. German scientists contributed to the development of advanced weapons systems and military technologies, propelling the U.S. ahead in the arms race with the Soviet Union. Their knowledge and expertise in fields like rocketry and missile technology were crucial in maintaining American military superiority.

Operation Paperclip also had a profound impact on medical advancements. German scientists brought their knowledge of human experimentation and medical research to the U.S., leading to significant breakthroughs in areas such as aerospace medicine and trauma surgery. However, the ethical controversies and moral dilemmas surrounding the use of data obtained from unethical experiments remain a contentious issue.

The involvement of German scientists in intelligence and espionage cannot be overlooked. Their expertise in encryption and code-breaking played a pivotal role in shaping American intelligence agencies' capabilities during the Cold War. Moreover, their contributions to the field of aeronautics facilitated advancements in reconnaissance and surveillance technologies.

Operation Paperclip's legacy extended to the field of aeronautics, where German scientists made significant contributions to the development of supersonic flight and stealth technology. Their expertise revolutionized the aviation industry, leading to advancements in aircraft design and performance.

Additionally, German scientists' involvement in nuclear research and chemical warfare had far-reaching implications. Their knowledge of nuclear physics contributed to the development of atomic weapons, while their expertise in chemical warfare influenced American military strategies and defensive measures.

Lastly, Operation Paperclip had an undisclosed impact on cybersecurity and cryptography. German scientists' understanding of encryption and cryptographic systems proved invaluable in safeguarding American communication networks and developing secure information systems.

In conclusion, the transfer of German technological expertise to the U.S. through Operation Paperclip had a profound and lasting impact across various fields. From space exploration to medical advancements, intelligence and espionage to nuclear research, the contributions of German Nazi scientists shaped the trajectory of American technological dominance. However, the ethical controversies and moral dilemmas associated with their recruitment continue to be debated. Understanding these hidden aspects of Operation Paperclip provides valuable insights into the complex interplay between science, politics, and morality during a critical era in history.

Operation Paperclip's Impact on Military Technology

Operation Paperclip, the covert U.S. program that recruited German Nazi scientists, had a profound impact on military technology. This subchapter explores the significant contributions made by these scientists and engineers in various areas of military research and development.

One of the key areas where Operation Paperclip had a lasting impact was space exploration. The recruitment of renowned rocket scientist Wernher von Braun and his team revolutionized American rocketry. Their expertise in developing the V-2 rocket during World War II was instrumental in the establishment of NASA and the subsequent missions to the moon. The advancements made by these German scientists propelled the United States to the forefront of space technology during the Cold War.

Moreover, Operation Paperclip played a vital role in shaping Cold War technology. The recruitment of German scientists helped the U.S. gain a significant advantage over the Soviet Union in areas such as missile defense, radar technology, and jet propulsion. The knowledge and expertise brought by these scientists bolstered American military capabilities, ultimately contributing to the outcome of the Cold War.

Additionally, Operation Paperclip had a secret involvement in the arms race. The German scientists' expertise in weapon development and engineering significantly influenced American military technology. They played a crucial role in the development of advanced weaponry, including guided missiles, nuclear warheads, and chemical agents. These advancements had a profound impact on the balance of power during the Cold War.

Furthermore, Operation Paperclip's impact extended to medical advancements. The German scientists' expertise in human experimentation and medical research contributed to significant breakthroughs in areas such as trauma surgery, aerospace medicine, and the development of vaccines. Their knowledge and experience paved the way for advancements in military medicine, saving countless lives on the battlefield.

Operation Paperclip also played a role in intelligence and espionage. The recruitment of German scientists with experience in cryptography and intelligence gathering provided the U.S. with valuable insights into the workings of enemy intelligence agencies. This knowledge proved crucial in developing counterintelligence strategies and maintaining a technological edge in the field of espionage.

Despite its undeniable impact on military technology, Operation Paperclip also raised ethical controversies and moral dilemmas. The program's involvement with former Nazi scientists sparked debates about the United States' willingness to overlook war crimes and human rights abuses in exchange for scientific knowledge.

In conclusion, Operation Paperclip's impact on military technology cannot be overstated. The recruitment of German Nazi scientists had far-reaching effects on various aspects of military research and development. From space exploration to Cold War technology, from medical advancements to intelligence and espionage, the contributions made by these scientists continue to shape the field of military technology to this day.

The Role of German Scientists in the Arms Race

In the subchapter "The Role of German Scientists in the Arms Race," we delve into the significant contributions made by German Nazi scientists recruited through Operation Paperclip. These scientists, brought to the United States after World War II, played a crucial role in shaping the arms race and influencing Cold War technology.

Operation Paperclip, the covert U.S. program to recruit German Nazi scientists, aimed to harness the expertise and knowledge of these scientists for American interests. This program had a profound impact on various fields, including space exploration, Cold War technology, intelligence, and espionage.

One of the major areas where these German scientists made notable contributions was in space exploration. Under the guidance of scientists such as Wernher von Braun, the United States developed its first successful ballistic missiles and ultimately launched the Apollo program, which put a man on the moon. The invaluable expertise of these German scientists propelled American space exploration to new heights, giving the U.S. a significant advantage in the Cold War space race against the Soviet Union.

Furthermore, the involvement of German scientists recruited through Operation Paperclip influenced Cold War technology. Their knowledge and expertise in areas such as rocketry, aerospace engineering, and electronics played a crucial role in the development of advanced military technologies. These advancements included intercontinental ballistic missiles (ICBMs), nuclear weapons, and advanced surveillance systems, significantly impacting the balance of power during the Cold War.

The German scientists' involvement in the arms race also extended to the field of aeronautics. Through their expertise in aircraft design and propulsion systems, they contributed to the development of cutting-edge military aircraft. Their influence can be seen in the creation of supersonic jets and stealth technology, which revolutionized modern warfare.

However, the recruitment of German Nazi scientists through Operation Paperclip also raised ethical controversies and moral dilemmas. Critics argue that employing scientists involved in war crimes and crimes against humanity compromises the moral integrity of the United States. This continues to be a contentious issue among historians and scholars.

In conclusion, the role of German scientists recruited through Operation Paperclip in the arms race was pivotal. Their expertise and knowledge significantly influenced space exploration, Cold War technology, aeronautics, and intelligence. However, the ethical controversies surrounding their involvement continue to be a subject of debate among historians and scholars. Nonetheless, their contributions have left a lasting legacy in the fields of military technology, space exploration, and intelligence, shaping the course of history.

Cold War Espionage and Intelligence Gathering

During the Cold War, espionage and intelligence gathering played a crucial role in shaping the geopolitical landscape. This subchapter explores the fascinating connection between Operation Paperclip and the world of intelligence, shedding light on the covert operations that occurred during this period.

Operation Paperclip, the clandestine program that recruited German Nazi scientists, had a significant impact on intelligence and espionage efforts during the Cold War. The United States sought to gain a strategic advantage over the Soviet Union by harnessing the knowledge and expertise of these German scientists.

The recruitment of German scientists allowed the United States to establish a sophisticated intelligence network, as these individuals possessed valuable insights into the technological advancements made by the Nazis during World War II. Through Operation Paperclip, the U.S. was able to access classified information, including research on weapons, surveillance techniques, and encryption methods.

The German scientists, who were well-versed in the art of espionage, also played a crucial role in training American intelligence officers. They shared their expertise in covert operations, counterintelligence, and code-breaking, providing invaluable knowledge that helped the U.S. stay one step ahead of its Soviet adversaries.

One of the key areas where Operation Paperclip influenced intelligence gathering was in the field of cryptography. The German scientists brought with them advanced encryption techniques that were employed by the Nazis during the war. These techniques were adapted and refined by American intelligence agencies, enabling them to intercept and decipher Soviet communications, gaining vital insights into their plans and activities.

Furthermore, the German scientists' involvement in intelligence gathering extended beyond traditional methods. They also played a significant role in the development of cutting-edge surveillance technology, including advanced listening devices, spy satellites, and aerial reconnaissance systems. These technological advancements revolutionized the intelligence community, providing unprecedented capabilities to monitor and gather information on Soviet activities.

However, the involvement of Nazi scientists in intelligence and espionage operations also raised ethical controversies and moral dilemmas. Many of these scientists had dubious backgrounds, having participated in war crimes or human experimentation during the Nazi regime. The decision to recruit them was met with criticism, as it raised questions about the United States' moral integrity and the extent to which the ends justified the means.

In conclusion, the subchapter "Cold War Espionage and Intelligence Gathering" highlights the significant role played by Operation Paperclip in shaping intelligence and espionage efforts during the Cold War. The recruitment of German Nazi scientists provided the U.S. with invaluable knowledge, advanced technologies, and expertise that greatly influenced the intelligence community. However, it also brought forth ethical controversies and moral dilemmas that continue to be debated to this day.

Chapter 4: Operation Paperclip: The Secret Involvement in the Arms Race

German Scientists' Contributions to Weapons Development

Subchapter: German Scientists' Contributions to Weapons Development

The covert U.S. program known as Operation Paperclip holds a fascinating chapter in history, chronicling the recruitment of German Nazi scientists following World War II. This subchapter explores their significant contributions to weapons development, shedding light on the impact they had on the field.

Operation Paperclip played a pivotal role in the transfer of German scientific expertise to the United States. Among the recruited scientists were brilliant minds who had worked on advanced weaponry during the war. Their knowledge and experience proved invaluable in shaping the future of weapons technology.

German scientists brought with them a wealth of expertise in various areas, including rocketry, aeronautics, nuclear research, and chemical warfare. Their contributions were instrumental in fueling the arms race that emerged during the Cold War between the United States and the Soviet Union.

One of the most notable achievements of the German scientists was their involvement in the development of ballistic missiles. Led by Wernher von Braun, they laid the foundation for the United States' successful space exploration program. Their expertise in rocketry propelled the nation to new heights, culminating in the historic moon landing.

Furthermore, the German scientists' expertise in nuclear research facilitated advancements in weaponry, leading to the development of more powerful and efficient nuclear warheads. Their contributions significantly influenced the United States' military capabilities during the Cold War and shaped the balance of power between nations.

In addition to their contributions to traditional forms of warfare, German scientists also played a role in the development of chemical warfare techniques. Their knowledge and research in this field had both defensive and offensive implications, impacting the strategies employed by the United States during the Cold War.

The German scientists' involvement in weapons development was not without ethical controversies and moral dilemmas. The recruitment of former Nazi scientists raised questions about the United States' willingness to overlook the scientists' past actions in the pursuit of technological advancements.

In conclusion, the German scientists recruited through Operation Paperclip made significant contributions to weapons development. Their expertise in rocketry, nuclear research, aeronautics, and chemical warfare shaped the United States' military capabilities and influenced the arms race during the Cold War. However, their involvement also raised ethical concerns and highlighted the complex nature of scientific advancements in times of war. The legacy of Operation Paperclip in the field of weapons development remains a fascinating and controversial aspect of history.

The Ethical Dilemmas of Employing Former Nazi Scientists

In the aftermath of World War II, a covert program known as Operation Paperclip was initiated by the United States to recruit German Nazi scientists. This subchapter aims to delve into the ethical controversies and moral dilemmas that arose from this operation. Addressing a niche audience of historians and individuals interested in the various impacts of Operation Paperclip, it is essential to examine the ethical implications of employing former Nazi scientists.

One of the primary ethical dilemmas of Operation Paperclip was the question of whether it was justifiable to overlook the scientists' involvement in Nazi war crimes in exchange for their scientific expertise. Many of these scientists had participated in human experimentation, forced labor, and other atrocities during the war. The decision to employ them raised concerns about moral accountability and the potential for establishing a precedent that allowed war criminals to escape justice.

Furthermore, employing former Nazi scientists created a dilemma regarding the responsibility of the United States in perpetuating the ideology that these individuals had propagated. By providing them with opportunities to continue their scientific careers, the US inadvertently legitimized the actions of the Nazi regime and undermined efforts towards reconciliation and justice.

Another ethical dilemma revolved around the potential risks of employing these scientists. While the US sought to benefit from their knowledge and expertise, there were concerns that they could bring with them dangerous ideologies or compromised loyalties. These individuals had once sworn allegiance to Hitler and the Third Reich, raising questions about their true allegiances and the potential for espionage or sabotage.

Moreover, the decision to employ former Nazi scientists had broader implications for society. It sent a message that scientific achievements and progress justified overlooking war crimes and human rights abuses. This raised ethical questions about the prioritization of scientific advancements over moral accountability and human dignity.

In conclusion, the subchapter "The Ethical Dilemmas of Employing Former Nazi Scientists" explores the complex moral questions that arose from Operation Paperclip. Historians and individuals interested in the impacts of this covert program will gain insights into the ethical controversies surrounding the decision to employ former Nazi scientists.

By examining these ethical dilemmas, we can better understand the historical context and the profound consequences of Operation Paperclip on various fields, including space exploration, Cold War technology, medical advancements, intelligence, and more.

The Hidden Impact of Operation Paperclip on Nuclear Capabilities

Throughout the history of Operation Paperclip, the covert U.S. program to recruit German Nazi scientists, the impact on various fields of study has been widely discussed and analyzed. However, one area that has largely remained hidden from public scrutiny is the program's influence on nuclear capabilities. This subchapter aims to shed light on this lesser-known aspect of Operation Paperclip and uncover its hidden contribution to the development of nuclear technology.

Under Operation Paperclip, hundreds of German scientists, including some with expertise in nuclear research, were brought to the United States after World War II. These scientists, many of whom had worked on the German nuclear program, were instrumental in advancing the U.S. nuclear capabilities during the Cold War.

One of the most notable contributions of these German scientists was their involvement in the Manhattan Project, the top-secret U.S. initiative to develop atomic weapons. Their expertise in nuclear physics and engineering proved invaluable in accelerating the development of the atomic bomb. Their knowledge of German advances in nuclear research, including enrichment techniques and reactor designs, provided crucial insights to the American scientists.

Beyond their contributions to the Manhattan Project, the German scientists recruited through Operation Paperclip played a vital role in shaping the U.S. nuclear program in the following years. They were instrumental in the development and improvement of nuclear reactors, nuclear propulsion systems for submarines and aircraft carriers, and the advancement of nuclear power generation.

Their expertise also extended to the field of nuclear medicine, where they made significant contributions to the understanding and application of radioactive isotopes in diagnosis and treatment. Their knowledge and experience in nuclear physics allowed for groundbreaking advancements in medical imaging techniques, such as the development of positron emission tomography (PET) scans.

However, the involvement of German Nazi scientists in the U.S. nuclear program raises ethical controversies and moral dilemmas. Critics argue that by recruiting these scientists, the United States was indirectly condoning their involvement in war crimes and crimes against humanity. The legacy of Operation Paperclip in the field of nuclear capabilities is thus accompanied by these ethical debates.

In conclusion, while the impact of Operation Paperclip on various fields of study has been extensively discussed, its hidden contribution to nuclear capabilities remains largely overlooked. The German scientists recruited through this covert program played a crucial role in advancing the U.S. nuclear program, both in terms of weapons development and peaceful applications in medicine and energy. However, this hidden legacy is not without its ethical controversies, prompting historians to further explore the complex implications of Operation Paperclip on nuclear research and its broader impact on society.

The Arms Race and Operation Paperclip's Undisclosed Role

As historians continue to delve into the depths of Operation Paperclip, the covert U.S. program that recruited German Nazi scientists, a startling revelation has come to light - the program's undisclosed role in the arms race. While the program's primary objective was to harness the scientific knowledge of these German scientists for the benefit of the United

States, it inadvertently contributed to the intensification of the global arms race during the Cold War.

Operation Paperclip, initiated in the aftermath of World War II, aimed to recruit top German scientists, engineers, and technicians who had previously worked on advanced military projects for the Nazi regime. These individuals possessed invaluable knowledge and expertise in fields ranging from rocketry and aeronautics to nuclear research and chemical warfare. The United States, aware of the potential strategic advantage they could gain, sought to capitalize on this wealth of knowledge.

The impact of Operation Paperclip on the arms race was twofold. Firstly, it provided the United States with a significant technological advantage over the Soviet Union. German scientists, such as Wernher von Braun, who had developed the V-2 rocket for the Nazis, played a crucial role in the development of American intercontinental ballistic missiles (ICBMs). This technological leap allowed the U.S. to establish itself as a dominant force in the arms race, sparking a race for supremacy in missile technology between the two superpowers.

Secondly, the presence of these German scientists within the United States created a sense of urgency among Soviet leaders to recruit their own scientists and accelerate their own weapons programs. This led to a further escalation of the arms race, with both sides pouring resources into developing more advanced and destructive weapons. The competition between the U.S. and the Soviet Union became a matter of national pride and security, pushing the boundaries of scientific and technological advancements in the pursuit of military dominance.

However, the undisclosed role of Operation Paperclip in the arms race raises ethical controversies and moral dilemmas. By recruiting former Nazi scientists, the United States inadvertently overlooked their participation in war crimes and human rights abuses committed during the Nazi regime. This compromising decision has since sparked debates about the ethical implications of sacrificing justice for scientific progress.

In conclusion, the undisclosed role of Operation Paperclip in the arms race sheds light on the intricate web of covert operations and strategic maneuvers that characterized the Cold War era. As historians continue to unravel the legacy of Operation Paperclip, it becomes increasingly evident that its impact on the arms race was far-reaching and profound. This chapter aims to explore this hidden aspect of the program, shedding light on its influence on global power dynamics and the ethical controversies it has generated.

Chapter 5: Operation Paperclip: The Hidden Contribution to Medical Advancements

German Scientists' Expertise in Medical Research

In the aftermath of World War II, the United States initiated Operation Paperclip, a covert program aimed at recruiting German Nazi scientists. While the primary focus of the program was on the fields of space exploration, Cold War technology, arms race, intelligence, and aeronautics, a lesser-known aspect of Operation Paperclip was the significant contribution made by German scientists to the field of medical research.

The expertise of these German scientists greatly influenced and accelerated medical advancements in the post-war era. Their knowledge and skills in various disciplines, including biology, pharmacology, and physiology, proved invaluable in pushing the boundaries of medical science.

One notable area in which German scientists played a vital role was in the development of vaccines. Their expertise in virology and immunology helped drive advancements in vaccine research and production. Through their contributions, numerous vaccines were developed, saving countless lives and preventing the spread of deadly diseases.

Additionally, German scientists' expertise in pharmacology led to significant advancements in the development of new drugs and medications. Their understanding of chemical compounds and their effects on the human body paved the way for the creation of life-saving drugs, including antibiotics, antivirals, and painkillers. These breakthroughs revolutionized healthcare, improving the quality of life for millions of people worldwide.

Furthermore, German scientists' knowledge of physiology and anatomy played a crucial role in advancing surgical techniques. Their insights into the human body's intricacies and the development of innovative surgical procedures contributed to improved patient outcomes and reduced mortality rates.

However, the involvement of German Nazi scientists in medical research raises ethical controversies and moral dilemmas. Many of these scientists were complicit in war crimes and atrocities committed during the Nazi regime. The decision to recruit them for their expertise sparked debates about the responsibility of scientific advancement versus the accountability for past actions.

Despite the ethical concerns, the legacy of German scientists in the field of medical research cannot be denied. Their expertise and contributions have had a lasting impact on healthcare, saving lives and improving the well-being of people worldwide. As historians, it is essential to acknowledge and examine the complex and often controversial history of Operation Paperclip and its influence on medical advancements.

Operation Paperclip's Impact on Biomedical Science

Operation Paperclip, the covert U.S. program that recruited German Nazi scientists, had a profound impact on various fields of science and technology. One of the areas that witnessed significant developments as a result of this program was biomedical science. This subchapter explores the hidden contribution made by Operation Paperclip in advancing medical knowledge and the ethical controversies that emerged.

Under Operation Paperclip, numerous German scientists, including medical researchers, were brought to the United States. These scientists possessed valuable knowledge and expertise gained from their work in

Nazi Germany. With their arrival, American biomedical science witnessed a dramatic leap forward.

The German scientists, who were experts in fields such as pharmacology, physiology, and genetics, brought with them groundbreaking research and methodologies. Their expertise in areas like human experimentation and biological weapons research, though morally questionable, provided valuable insights that led to significant advancements in medical understanding.

One notable impact of Operation Paperclip on biomedical science was the advancement of pharmacology. German scientists had made considerable progress in the development of drugs and medications, and their knowledge greatly contributed to the improvement of pharmaceutical research in the United States. This ultimately led to the development of life-saving drugs and treatments for various diseases.

Furthermore, the German scientists' expertise in physiology and genetics played a crucial role in furthering our understanding of the human body. Their research helped pave the way for breakthroughs in areas such as organ transplantation, genetic engineering, and the study of hereditary diseases. The knowledge and techniques brought by these scientists greatly accelerated biomedical research, benefiting not only the United States but also the global scientific community.

However, the involvement of Nazi scientists in Operation Paperclip also raised significant ethical controversies and moral dilemmas. The scientists' past involvement in human experimentation and their association with the atrocities committed during World War II sparked widespread debate. Critics argued that by employing these scientists, the United States was indirectly condoning their actions and undermining the principles of justice and accountability.

In conclusion, Operation Paperclip had a significant impact on biomedical science. The recruitment of German Nazi scientists brought invaluable knowledge and expertise, leading to remarkable advancements in pharmacology, physiology, and genetics. While their contributions accelerated medical research, the ethical controversies surrounding their involvement remain an important topic for historians to explore and understand.

Medical Discoveries and Breakthroughs Stemming from Operation Paperclip

Operation Paperclip, the covert U.S. program that recruited German Nazi scientists after World War II, had far-reaching effects in various fields, including medicine. The program, aimed at leveraging the scientific knowledge and expertise of former Nazi scientists, led to numerous medical discoveries and breakthroughs that continue to shape the field of medicine today.

One of the significant contributions resulting from Operation Paperclip was the advancement in the understanding and treatment of infectious diseases. German scientists brought their expertise in virology and bacteriology, which proved invaluable in combating diseases such as tuberculosis, polio, and influenza. Their research and discoveries paved the way for the development of vaccines and antiviral medications, saving countless lives.

Furthermore, Operation Paperclip played a crucial role in the field of pharmacology and drug development. German scientists familiar with the production of chemical compounds and pharmaceuticals revolutionized the pharmaceutical industry. They introduced new techniques and methodologies for synthesizing drugs, leading to the development of life-saving medications for various conditions, including cardiovascular diseases, cancer, and mental illnesses.

The medical advancements resulting from Operation Paperclip also extended to surgical procedures and techniques. German scientists brought innovative ideas and technologies, such as the use of microsurgery, which allowed for intricate and precise surgical interventions. This breakthrough in surgical techniques has significantly improved patient outcomes and revolutionized the field of surgery.

Additionally, the knowledge and expertise of former Nazi scientists had a significant impact on the field of neurology and neuroscience. Their research on the human brain and nervous system laid the foundation for understanding neurological disorders and developing treatments for conditions such as epilepsy, Alzheimer's disease, and Parkinson's disease.

Although Operation Paperclip undeniably contributed to several medical breakthroughs, it also raises ethical controversies and moral dilemmas. The program involved recruiting scientists who had actively participated in Nazi atrocities, prompting debates on the ethics of employing individuals with such backgrounds. The legacy of Operation Paperclip in the medical field is thus intertwined with these ethical considerations.

In conclusion, the covert U.S. program Operation Paperclip had a profound impact on medical advancements. The recruitment of German Nazi scientists led to significant breakthroughs in infectious diseases, pharmacology, surgery, and neurology. However, the ethical controversies surrounding the program cannot be ignored, highlighting the complex nature of the legacy of Operation Paperclip in the field of medicine.

The Controversy Surrounding Human Experimentation

Human experimentation is a topic that has stirred up significant controversy throughout history. This subchapter aims to delve into the ethical controversies and moral dilemmas surrounding human experimentation, specifically within the context of Operation Paperclip.

Operation Paperclip, the covert U.S. program that recruited German Nazi scientists following World War II, has been widely known for its role in advancing space exploration, Cold War technology, medical advancements, intelligence, and espionage. However, the program's involvement in human experimentation raises serious ethical questions.

Under the Nazi regime, German scientists conducted heinous experiments on prisoners in concentration camps, including inhumane medical procedures, testing the limits of human endurance, and researching biological warfare. Operation Paperclip allowed some of these scientists to continue their research in the United States, which ignited a heated debate among historians and scholars.

Critics argue that by recruiting these scientists, the U.S. government was turning a blind eye to their past atrocities and effectively granting them impunity. They argue that these scientists should have been held accountable for their crimes rather than being rewarded with prestigious positions in American institutions.

Furthermore, the utilization of data obtained through unethical means raises concerns about the legitimacy and validity of the research. The question arises: can we trust the findings and contributions of scientists who have a tainted past?

Proponents of Operation Paperclip, on the other hand, argue that the ends justified the means. By harnessing the knowledge and expertise of these German scientists, the United States gained a significant advantage in various fields, including aeronautics, nuclear research, chemical warfare, and cybersecurity.

Nevertheless, the controversy surrounding human experimentation cannot be easily dismissed. It forces us to confront difficult questions

                    ROBERTO MIGUEL RODRIGUEZ

about the balance between scientific progress and ethical responsibility. How can we ensure that the pursuit of knowledge does not come at the cost of human dignity? Do the contributions made by these scientists outweigh their past actions? Is it possible to separate a scientist's professional achievements from their personal moral compass?

As historians, it is our duty to critically analyze the impact of Operation Paperclip and its ethical implications. By exploring the controversies surrounding human experimentation within this context, we shed light on a dark chapter in history and stimulate further discussion on the delicate balance between scientific advancement and ethical considerations.

Chapter 6: Operation Paperclip: The Role in Intelligence and Espionage

The Recruitment of German Intelligence Specialists

One aspect often overlooked in the extensive discussions surrounding Operation Paperclip and its recruitment of German Nazi scientists is the role played by German intelligence specialists. These individuals, with their vast expertise in espionage and intelligence gathering, were an invaluable asset to the covert U.S. program.

Under Operation Paperclip, the United States sought to harness the scientific and technological prowess of German scientists, including those with ties to the Nazi regime, in order to gain an advantage in the post-World War II era. However, it was not just their scientific knowledge that interested the U.S. intelligence agencies; it was their experience in intelligence operations that proved equally valuable.

German intelligence specialists brought with them a wealth of knowledge in the field of espionage and counterintelligence. Having operated under the Nazi regime, these specialists were well-versed in the tactics and techniques employed by the German intelligence apparatus. This knowledge was crucial in helping the United States understand and counter the intelligence operations of potential adversaries, such as the Soviet Union.

Moreover, the recruitment of German intelligence specialists also provided the U.S. with a unique opportunity to establish a network of informants and agents within the Soviet Union and other communist countries. These specialists had extensive contacts and networks within the intelligence community, which they could leverage to gather vital information. Their expertise in clandestine operations and intelligence analysis proved instrumental in shaping U.S. intelligence efforts during the Cold War.

The recruitment of German intelligence specialists also had a significant impact on the field of cryptography and cybersecurity. The Nazis, particularly the infamous Enigma machine, had developed sophisticated encryption techniques that posed a significant challenge to Allied intelligence operations during World War II. By recruiting German intelligence specialists, the U.S. gained access to their knowledge of encryption methods and cryptographic systems, allowing for advancements in code-breaking and the development of more secure communication systems.

However, the recruitment of German intelligence specialists under Operation Paperclip also raises ethical controversies and moral dilemmas. Many of these individuals had been active participants in the Nazi regime's intelligence operations, and their actions had caused immense harm and suffering. Critics argue that by employing these individuals, the United States was condoning their past actions and undermining the principles of justice.

In conclusion, the recruitment of German intelligence specialists played a crucial role in Operation Paperclip and its covert U.S. program to recruit German Nazi scientists. Their expertise in espionage and intelligence gathering provided the U.S. with invaluable insights into enemy intelligence operations and helped shape U.S. intelligence efforts during the Cold War. However, the ethical controversies surrounding their recruitment highlight the complex nature of Operation Paperclip and its legacy in the field of intelligence and espionage.

Operation Paperclip's Influence on Cold War Intelligence Operations

Operation Paperclip was a covert U.S. program that aimed to recruit German Nazi scientists following World War II. This subchapter will delve into the profound influence this operation had on Cold War intelligence operations. Historians and those interested in the intricacies of Operation Paperclip will find this exploration enlightening.

One of the primary reasons for the recruitment of German scientists under Operation Paperclip was to gain an advantage over the Soviet Union in the emerging Cold War. The United States recognized the need to bolster its intelligence capabilities to counter the Soviet threat, and the expertise of these German scientists was seen as invaluable in achieving this goal.

The integration of these scientists into the U.S. intelligence community had a significant impact. Many of them were experts in fields such as physics, chemistry, and engineering, which were crucial to the development of advanced intelligence technologies. Their knowledge and skills were utilized in the creation of cutting-edge surveillance systems, code-breaking techniques, and communication interception methods.

These German scientists also played a pivotal role in the establishment of intelligence agencies such as the National Security Agency (NSA) and the Central Intelligence Agency (CIA). Their expertise in cryptography and espionage techniques greatly contributed to the intelligence community's ability to gather and decipher information during the Cold War.

Furthermore, Operation Paperclip had a profound impact on the field of counterintelligence. The German scientists brought with them a wealth of knowledge regarding the tactics and strategies employed by the Nazi regime. This insight proved invaluable in understanding and countering Soviet intelligence activities.

However, the involvement of former Nazi scientists in U.S. intelligence operations also raised ethical controversies and moral dilemmas. Many of these scientists had been complicit in war crimes and atrocities committed by the Nazi regime. This led to debates about the extent to which their past actions should be overlooked in the interest of national security.

In conclusion, Operation Paperclip had a far-reaching influence on Cold War intelligence operations. The recruitment of German Nazi scientists significantly bolstered the U.S. intelligence community's capabilities, leading to advancements in surveillance technology, code-breaking techniques, and counterintelligence strategies. However, the ethical controversies surrounding the program continue to be a subject of debate amongst historians and scholars.

Espionage and Counterintelligence Efforts Involving German Scientists

The subchapter titled "Espionage and Counterintelligence Efforts Involving German Scientists" delves into the covert operations and intelligence activities surrounding the recruitment of German Nazi scientists in Operation Paperclip. This chapter aims to provide historians and enthusiasts of Operation Paperclip with a comprehensive understanding of the espionage and counterintelligence efforts associated with the program.

Operation Paperclip, the covert U.S. program to recruit German Nazi scientists, was not merely a scientific venture but also a strategic move in the Cold War era. The United States, recognizing the value of German scientific expertise, sought to gain an advantage over the Soviet Union by acquiring German scientists and their knowledge. However, this posed significant challenges in terms of espionage and counterintelligence.

To prevent the Soviet Union from gaining access to these scientists and their research, elaborate measures were put in place. The U.S. government established a rigorous screening process to identify potential security risks among the German scientists. Intelligence agencies closely monitored their activities, communications, and interactions to ensure they did not engage in any espionage or share classified information with foreign powers.

Additionally, a network of intelligence officers and counterintelligence agents was deployed to gather information on the Soviet Union's attempts to recruit German scientists. These efforts included surveillance, wiretapping, and undercover operations, all aimed at identifying and neutralizing any threats to U.S. national security.

The subchapter also explores the role of the German scientists themselves in intelligence and espionage activities. Some scientists, driven by personal or ideological motivations, engaged in espionage on behalf of the United States. They provided valuable information on Soviet scientific advancements, military capabilities, and espionage activities, further heightening the intelligence war between the two superpowers.

However, this subchapter does not shy away from addressing the ethical controversies and moral dilemmas surrounding Operation Paperclip. The recruitment of German scientists who had been associated with the Nazi regime raised questions about the United States' willingness to overlook their past actions in the pursuit of scientific knowledge and national advantage.

Overall, this subchapter sheds light on the intricate web of espionage and counterintelligence efforts surrounding Operation Paperclip. It underscores the critical role these efforts played in safeguarding U.S. national security interests, while also acknowledging the ethical dilemmas inherent in the recruitment of German Nazi scientists. By providing a comprehensive account of espionage and counterintelligence, this chapter contributes to a deeper understanding of Operation Paperclip's impact on intelligence, technology, and the Cold War era as a whole.

The Ethical Implications of Collaborating with Former Nazi Spies

In the realm of Operation Paperclip, a covert U.S. program that recruited German Nazi scientists, there lies a dark and controversial aspect that historians must confront – the ethical implications of collaborating with former Nazi spies. This subchapter aims to shed light on the moral dilemmas and controversies that surround this topic, as it pertains to the various niches within Operation Paperclip.

When the United States embarked on Operation Paperclip, its objective was clear – to harness the scientific knowledge and expertise of German scientists for American advancement. However, in doing so, they found themselves grappling with a profound ethical quandary – should they collaborate with former Nazi spies, individuals who had actively participated in heinous crimes against humanity?

For historians studying Operation Paperclip, these ethical implications present a complex and multifaceted dilemma. On one hand, the knowledge and expertise possessed by these former Nazi spies were invaluable to the fields of space exploration, Cold War technology, medical advancements, intelligence, aeronautics, nuclear research, chemical warfare, and even cybersecurity and cryptography. Their contributions in these areas undoubtedly propelled the United States forward, solidifying its position as a global superpower.

However, the collaboration with former Nazi spies raises questions about the moral responsibility of the United States. By welcoming these individuals into their scientific community, were they inadvertently condoning and rewarding their past actions? Should the pursuit of scientific advancement override the need for justice and accountability?

Moreover, the ethical implications of collaborating with former Nazi spies extend beyond the immediate consequences. The legacy of Operation Paperclip lingers, casting a shadow on the achievements and advancements made possible by these scientists. The knowledge and expertise gained from these collaborations must be critically examined and contextualized within the troubling historical backdrop of Nazi Germany.

Ultimately, historians must grapple with the ethical dilemmas presented by Operation Paperclip, recognizing the moral complexities that arise when scientific progress collides with the crimes of the past. As the field delves deeper into the hidden chapters of history, it is essential to engage in critical discourse, shedding light on the choices made and the ramifications they continue to have on our understanding of morality, justice, and the pursuit of knowledge.

Chapter 7: Operation Paperclip: The Ethical Controversies and Moral Dilemmas

The Debate Over Granting Immunity to Former Nazi Scientists

In the aftermath of World War II, when the United States found itself in a fierce Cold War rivalry with the Soviet Union, a covert program named Operation Paperclip was initiated. Its objective was to recruit German Nazi scientists, engineers, and technicians who had been involved in the development of advanced technology and scientific research during the war. The program aimed to leverage their expertise and knowledge for the benefit of the United States.

Operation Paperclip, however, was not without its ethical controversies and moral dilemmas. One of the most contentious issues was whether to grant immunity to these former Nazi scientists, knowing their involvement in crimes against humanity.

The debate over granting immunity revolved around several key arguments. On one hand, proponents argued that these scientists possessed invaluable knowledge and experience that could significantly advance various fields, such as space exploration, aeronautics, nuclear research, and intelligence. They believed that by providing immunity, the United States could tap into this expertise and gain a strategic advantage over its Cold War adversary.

On the other hand, critics argued that granting immunity to former Nazi scientists was an affront to justice and morality. They questioned the ethical implications of absolving individuals who had actively participated in the Nazi regime's atrocities, including human experimentation, chemical warfare, and involvement in the Holocaust. Granting immunity, they argued, would send a message that such crimes could be overlooked in the pursuit of technological and scientific advancements.

The debate also extended to the potential consequences of Operation Paperclip on the international stage. Some historians argue that the program's secret involvement in the arms race and its undisclosed impact on cybersecurity and cryptography had far-reaching implications. Others believe that the legacy of Operation Paperclip in the field of aeronautics, space exploration, medical advancements, and intelligence was significant and undeniable.

Ultimately, the decision to grant immunity to former Nazi scientists was a complex and multifaceted one. It required weighing the benefits of their knowledge against the ethical concerns of their past actions. Operation Paperclip remains a controversial chapter in history, highlighting the difficult choices made in the pursuit of scientific and technological progress during a tumultuous era.

Public Perception and Media Coverage of Operation Paperclip

Operation Paperclip, the covert U.S. program that recruited German Nazi scientists, remains a subject of fascination and controversy among historians and various niches. The public perception and media coverage of this operation have played a significant role in shaping the narrative surrounding it.

From its inception in the aftermath of World War II, Operation Paperclip has attracted both praise and criticism. Media coverage during the early years of the program focused on the perceived necessity of recruiting German scientists to gain a technological advantage in the escalating Cold War. The media portrayed these scientists as essential to the United States' efforts to surpass the Soviet Union in areas such as space exploration, nuclear research, and aeronautics.

However, as details about the Nazi past of some of these scientists began to emerge, public perception shifted. The media started to question the ethical controversies and moral dilemmas associated with the program. Journalists highlighted the involvement of Operation Paperclip scientists in heinous crimes committed during the war, such as human experimentation or their role in chemical warfare. These revelations sparked public outcry and calls for accountability.

Over time, the media coverage also shed light on the hidden contributions made by Operation Paperclip scientists to various fields. Reports emerged on their involvement in medical advancements, intelligence and espionage, and even cybersecurity and cryptography. These revelations challenged the simplistic narrative of Operation Paperclip as a black-and-white issue and forced the public to grapple with the complex legacy of these scientists.

The public perception of Operation Paperclip has evolved over the years, shaped by the media coverage and the ongoing research conducted by historians. This subchapter aims to analyze and dissect the various aspects of this perception, from the initial positive portrayal to the subsequent ethical controversies and the undisclosed impact on different fields of study.

By examining the historical context, media coverage, and public sentiment surrounding Operation Paperclip, historians can gain a comprehensive understanding of the program's complexities. This subchapter provides a platform for historians to delve into the public perception and media coverage of Operation Paperclip, allowing for a more nuanced understanding of its legacy and impact on various fields.

Criticisms of Operation Paperclip's Lack of Accountability

Throughout history, Operation Paperclip has been both praised and criticized for its covert program that recruited German Nazi scientists.

While many historians acknowledge the positive impact of this operation on various fields, there are legitimate criticisms of its lack of accountability.

One of the main criticisms of Operation Paperclip is the lack of thorough background checks conducted on the scientists. In their haste to acquire German scientific expertise, the U.S. government overlooked the Nazi past of some of these scientists. This lack of accountability raises ethical questions about whether it was appropriate to grant immunity to individuals who had actively participated in Nazi war crimes.

Another criticism is the secrecy surrounding Operation Paperclip. The covert nature of the program meant that the American public and even Congress were largely kept in the dark about the recruitment of former Nazi scientists. This lack of transparency eroded public trust and created an atmosphere of suspicion.

Furthermore, Operation Paperclip's lack of accountability extended to the scientists themselves. Many of them were given high-ranking positions within the U.S. government and military, without facing any consequences for their actions during World War II. This lack of accountability allowed some scientists to continue their unethical research practices or maintain their allegiance to Nazi ideologies.

The impact of Operation Paperclip on the arms race is another area of criticism. By recruiting German scientists, the U.S. gained access to advanced technology and intelligence. However, this also meant that former Nazi scientists were contributing to the development of weapons of mass destruction. Critics argue that this compromises the moral high ground that the U.S. claimed during the Cold War.

Additionally, Operation Paperclip's lack of accountability raises concerns about the long-term legacy of the program. By allowing former Nazi scientists to continue their work, the U.S. indirectly endorsed their actions and ideologies. This raises questions about the moral dilemmas faced by the American government and the potential negative consequences of this decision.

In conclusion, while Operation Paperclip undoubtedly had a significant impact on various fields, it is crucial to acknowledge and address its lack of accountability. Historians must critically examine the ethical controversies and moral dilemmas surrounding this covert program. By doing so, we can gain a more comprehensive understanding of the legacy and implications of Operation Paperclip in the context of the broader historical narrative.

The Long-Term Implications on Historical Memory and Justice

In the subchapter titled "The Long-Term Implications on Historical Memory and Justice," we delve into the profound impact of Operation Paperclip on the collective memory of history and the pursuit of justice. Historians, who have dedicated their lives to understanding and documenting the past, play a crucial role in unraveling the complex consequences of this covert U.S. program.

Operation Paperclip: Unveiling the Covert U.S. Program that Recruited German Nazi Scientists sheds light on the hidden truths surrounding the recruitment of German Nazi scientists in the aftermath of World War II. This book addresses the niches of Operation Paperclip, providing historians with comprehensive insights into its various aspects.

One of the significant long-term implications of Operation Paperclip is the distortion of historical memory. By employing Nazi scientists responsible for heinous crimes against humanity, the United States inadvertently altered the narrative surrounding World War II and the Holocaust. The inclusion of these scientists in the American scientific community obscured their wartime activities, leaving a gap in the historical record. Historians must grapple with the challenge of reconciling the contributions made by these individuals with the atrocities they committed or enabled.

Furthermore, Operation Paperclip poses a fundamental question about justice. The decision to recruit Nazi scientists raises ethical controversies and moral dilemmas. Historians must explore whether the desire for technological advancement and geopolitical advantage justified overlooking war crimes and human rights violations. This subchapter delves into the intricacies of these debates, shedding light on the ethical considerations that influenced the program's architects and the consequences of their choices.

Moreover, by examining the long-term effects of Operation Paperclip, historians can uncover its hidden legacy in various fields. From space exploration to aeronautics, nuclear research to intelligence and espionage, the impact of these German scientists' contributions cannot be understated. This subchapter explores the lasting influence of Operation Paperclip on Cold War technology, the arms race, medical advancements, chemical warfare, cybersecurity, and cryptography.

In conclusion, "The Long-Term Implications on Historical Memory and Justice" subchapter within Operation Paperclip: Unveiling the Covert U.S. Program that Recruited German Nazi Scientists is an essential resource for historians. It examines the distortion of historical memory, explores the ethical controversies surrounding justice, and uncovers the hidden legacy of Operation Paperclip in various fields. By critically analyzing this covert program, historians can contribute to a more accurate understanding of the past and its enduring consequences.

Chapter 8: Operation Paperclip: The Legacy in the Field of Aeronautics

German Scientists' Influence on Aeronautical Engineering

Aeronautical engineering, the field that deals with the development and design of aircraft, has been greatly influenced by the contributions of German scientists. During World War II, the United States initiated a covert program called Operation Paperclip to recruit German Nazi scientists, including those involved in aeronautical research. This subchapter explores the significant impact these scientists had on the field of aeronautical engineering.

One of the most notable German scientists recruited under Operation Paperclip was Wernher von Braun, a pioneer in rocketry and space exploration. Von Braun's expertise in rocket propulsion led to the development of the V-2 rocket, which laid the foundation for future space travel. After the war, Von Braun played a crucial role in the development of the Saturn V rocket, which enabled the United States to reach the moon during the Apollo missions.

Another influential figure was Hans von Ohain, a German engineer who developed the world's first operational jet engine. His work revolutionized aviation by providing faster and more efficient means of propulsion. Von Ohain's contributions paved the way for the development of supersonic aircraft, such as the famous Concorde, and laid the groundwork for modern aviation technology.

In addition to propulsion, German scientists also made significant advancements in aerodynamics. Ludwig Prandtl, known as the father of modern aerodynamics, introduced the concept of boundary layers and developed theories that improved the efficiency and performance of aircraft. His research on wing profiles and drag reduction techniques greatly influenced the design of airplanes, making them more maneuverable and fuel-efficient.

The influence of German scientists on aeronautical engineering extended beyond the development of aircraft. Their expertise in materials science and structural engineering led to innovations in aircraft construction, resulting in safer and more robust designs. For instance, the use of composite materials in aircraft construction, pioneered by German scientists, significantly reduced the weight of aircraft while maintaining their structural integrity.

The contributions of German scientists to aeronautical engineering have had a lasting impact on the field. Their expertise in propulsion, aerodynamics, and aircraft construction has shaped modern aviation technology, enabling safer and more efficient air travel. The legacy of these scientists continues to inspire advancements in aeronautical engineering and serves as a testament to the complex ethical controversies and moral dilemmas surrounding Operation Paperclip.

Operation Paperclip's Impact on Aircraft Design and Technology

Operation Paperclip, the covert U.S. program that recruited German Nazi scientists, had a profound impact on various fields of study and technology. One area where its influence was particularly significant was in aircraft design and technology. This subchapter explores the contributions of Operation Paperclip scientists in revolutionizing aeronautics and shaping the future of aviation.

Under Operation Paperclip, numerous German scientists with expertise in aircraft design and technology were brought to the United States. These scientists, who had previously worked on advanced aircraft projects for the Nazi regime, now found themselves contributing to the American aviation industry. Their knowledge and expertise played a crucial role in advancing aircraft technology beyond what was previously imaginable.

One notable impact of Operation Paperclip was the development of high-speed aircraft. German scientists brought their expertise in aerodynamics and propulsion systems, enabling the United States to make significant advancements in supersonic flight. Through their contributions, American engineers were able to design and build aircraft that could break the sound barrier, leading to the development of iconic planes like the Bell X-1.

Additionally, Operation Paperclip scientists played a vital role in the development of stealth technology. German engineers, such as those from the Horten brothers' team, brought their expertise in designing aircraft with reduced radar cross-sections. This knowledge paved the way for the creation of stealth aircraft like the F-117 Nighthawk and the B-2 Spirit, which revolutionized modern warfare.

Furthermore, the German scientists' contributions to aircraft design and technology had a lasting impact on the field of aeronautics. Their expertise in areas such as jet propulsion, aerodynamics, and materials science pushed the boundaries of what was possible in aviation. Their advancements led to the development of more efficient and capable aircraft, improving speed, range, and maneuverability.

In conclusion, Operation Paperclip had a significant impact on aircraft design and technology. The recruitment of German scientists with expertise in aviation propelled the United States to the forefront of aeronautical innovation. Their contributions in areas such as high-speed flight, stealth technology, and overall advancements in aircraft design transformed the field of aviation and set the stage for future breakthroughs. The legacy of Operation Paperclip in the realm of aeronautics remains undeniable, forever shaping the course of aviation history.

The Continued Influence of German Scientists in Modern Aviation

Germans have long been known for their contributions to the field of aviation, and this influence has continued to shape modern aircraft technology. Operation Paperclip, the covert U.S. program that recruited German Nazi Scientists after World War II, played a significant role in bringing this knowledge to America. Historians and enthusiasts of Operation Paperclip recognize the profound impact these German scientists had on various niches, including the field of aeronautics.

The legacy of Operation Paperclip's German scientists in aviation can be seen in several key areas. First and foremost, their expertise in aircraft design and aerodynamics brought about significant advancements that continue to shape modern aircraft. The Germans' understanding of streamlining, wing design, and propulsion systems proved invaluable in improving the speed, efficiency, and safety of airplanes.

One notable example is the influence of Wernher von Braun, a prominent German scientist who was instrumental in the development of the V-2 rocket during the war. After being brought to the United States through Operation Paperclip, von Braun's expertise in rocketry laid the foundation for the American space program. His work on the Saturn V rocket, which powered the Apollo missions to the moon, showcased the direct impact of German scientists on space exploration.

Furthermore, German scientists recruited through Operation Paperclip also contributed to the advancement of aviation technology during the Cold War. Their expertise in radar systems, navigation, and missile guidance systems directly influenced the development of military aircraft and weapon systems. The German scientists' knowledge and experience were vital in shaping the technological landscape of the era, leading to improved reconnaissance capabilities and enhanced military aircraft performance.

In addition to military applications, Operation Paperclip's German scientists made significant contributions to civil aviation. Their knowledge of aircraft materials and structures allowed for the development of safer and more efficient aircraft designs. For instance, their work on lightweight materials, such as carbon composites, revolutionized the aerospace industry by reducing the weight of aircraft and improving fuel efficiency.

The continued influence of German scientists recruited through Operation Paperclip in modern aviation cannot be overstated. Their expertise and contributions in aircraft design, propulsion systems, space exploration, military applications, and civil aviation have shaped the field for decades. Understanding their legacy provides valuable insights into the transformation of aviation technology and its impact on various niches, from space exploration to the arms race, medical advancements to intelligence and espionage. Operation Paperclip, with its ethical controversies and moral dilemmas, leaves a lasting mark on the field of aeronautics and serves as a reminder of the complex relationship between scientific progress and historical events.

The Ethical Considerations of Benefitting from Former Nazi Expertise

The covert U.S. program known as Operation Paperclip, which aimed to recruit German Nazi scientists following World War II, remains a topic of great interest and controversy among historians. This subchapter delves into the ethical considerations surrounding the program, examining the moral dilemmas faced by the United States as they sought to benefit from the expertise of former Nazi scientists.

Operation Paperclip had a significant impact on various fields, including space exploration, Cold War technology, medical advancements, intelligence and espionage, aeronautics, nuclear research, chemical warfare, cybersecurity, and cryptography. While the program undoubtedly contributed to advancements in these areas, it raises important questions about the ethical implications of collaborating with individuals who were responsible for heinous crimes during the war.

One of the primary ethical concerns of Operation Paperclip is the issue of moral responsibility. Should the United States have allowed former Nazi scientists, who may have been directly involved in war crimes and atrocities, to escape punishment and instead benefit from their knowledge? This question challenges our understanding of justice and accountability, as well as the extent to which the ends justify the means.

Furthermore, Operation Paperclip raised questions about the potential whitewashing of Nazi crimes. By integrating these scientists into American society and providing them with prestigious positions and honors, the U.S. inadvertently contributed to the rehabilitation of individuals who had actively supported a regime responsible for genocide and other human rights abuses. This aspect of the program highlights the moral dilemma of prioritizing scientific advancements over confronting the past and acknowledging the horrors of the Nazi regime.

The ethical complexities of Operation Paperclip also extend to the broader implications of using technology and knowledge obtained from former Nazi scientists. How should society view advancements made possible by individuals with a dark past? Can we separate the knowledge from the person who created it? These questions touch upon the responsibility of scientists, scholars, and society as a whole in grappling with the legacy of Operation Paperclip.

In conclusion, the ethical considerations surrounding Operation Paperclip are profound and multifaceted. The program's impact on various fields cannot be denied, but it raises important moral dilemmas and controversies that continue to be debated by historians. As we explore the legacy of Operation Paperclip, it is crucial to engage in thoughtful reflection on the ethical implications of benefiting from former Nazi expertise, recognizing the complexities and challenges it presents to our understanding of justice, accountability, and the pursuit of scientific progress.

Chapter 9: Operation Paperclip: The German Scientists' Influence on Nuclear Research

The Role of German Scientists in the Development of Nuclear Weapons

Operation Paperclip: Unveiling the Covert U.S. Program that Recruited German Nazi Scientists

As historians, it is our duty to uncover the truth behind historical events and shed light on lesser-known aspects of significant moments in history. In this subchapter, we delve into the role of German scientists in the development of nuclear weapons, specifically within the context of Operation Paperclip, the covert U.S. program that recruited German Nazi scientists.

Operation Paperclip, initiated in the aftermath of World War II, aimed to harness the scientific expertise of German scientists for the benefit of the United States. Among these scientists were individuals who had played crucial roles in Germany's nuclear research and weapons programs. Their knowledge became invaluable to the U.S. as it sought to establish itself as a nuclear power during the early years of the Cold War.

Under Operation Paperclip, German scientists such as Wernher von Braun, Kurt Diebner, and Otto Hahn were brought to the United States. These scientists had made significant contributions to nuclear research, including advancements in the field of nuclear fission and the development of the first operational ballistic missile, the V-2 rocket. Their expertise proved instrumental in the U.S. efforts to develop its own nuclear arsenal and improve its missile technology.

The influence of these German scientists extended beyond the development of nuclear weapons. Their knowledge and expertise also contributed to advancements in space exploration, aeronautics, and intelligence and espionage. Through their involvement in Operation Paperclip, the U.S. gained access to valuable information that propelled its scientific and technological capabilities to new heights.

However, the legacy of Operation Paperclip is not without ethical controversies and moral dilemmas. The program's recruitment of Nazi scientists, some of whom had been involved in heinous war crimes, raised questions about the ethics of employing individuals with such backgrounds. These concerns continue to be debated among historians and scholars to this day.

In conclusion, the role of German scientists in the development of nuclear weapons cannot be overlooked, particularly within the context of Operation Paperclip. Their knowledge and expertise significantly contributed to the U.S.'s advancements in nuclear research, space exploration, and intelligence operations. However, the ethical controversies surrounding the program should not be ignored, as they remind us of the complex and often morally ambiguous decisions made in the pursuit of scientific and technological progress.

Operation Paperclip's Contribution to Nuclear Research Programs

Operation Paperclip, the covert U.S. program that recruited German Nazi scientists, had a profound impact on various fields, including nuclear research programs. This subchapter delves into the specific contributions made by Operation Paperclip to the advancement of nuclear research, shedding light on its significance and implications.

The program, initiated in the aftermath of World War II, aimed to harness the scientific knowledge and expertise of German Nazi scientists for the benefit of the United States. Many of these scientists, including renowned figures like Wernher von Braun and Kurt Diebner, had extensive experience in nuclear research and were instrumental in the development of Germany's nuclear program during the war.

Under Operation Paperclip, these scientists were brought to the United States and integrated into the country's scientific community. Their expertise and knowledge played a pivotal role in advancing nuclear research programs in the post-war era. They provided valuable insights into various aspects of nuclear science, including nuclear physics, reactor design, and the development of nuclear weapons.

One of the key contributions of Operation Paperclip in the field of nuclear research was its impact on the Manhattan Project. The knowledge and expertise of the German scientists greatly accelerated the project's progress, leading to the successful development of the atomic bomb. Their insights and technical skills enabled the United States to become a nuclear superpower, fundamentally altering the course of history.

Furthermore, Operation Paperclip's contribution to nuclear research extended beyond weapons development. The German scientists brought critical insights into peaceful applications of nuclear energy, such as nuclear power generation and medical advancements. Their expertise in nuclear physics and reactor design laid the foundation for the development of nuclear power plants, which continue to play a significant role in the world's energy production.

Moreover, the German scientists' involvement in Operation Paperclip had far-reaching implications for the Cold War era. Their knowledge of nuclear technology and weapons development shaped the arms race between the United States and the Soviet Union. The race for nuclear superiority would have been drastically different without the contributions of these scientists, who provided valuable insights into nuclear weapon design, testing, and delivery systems.

In conclusion, Operation Paperclip's recruitment of German Nazi scientists had a profound impact on nuclear research programs. The contributions made by these scientists in the fields of nuclear physics, reactor design, and weapons development were invaluable. Their expertise not only propelled the United States to the forefront of nuclear technology but also had significant implications for the Cold War, energy production, and medical advancements. Understanding the role of Operation Paperclip in nuclear research provides a comprehensive perspective on the program's influence and sheds light on its complex legacy.

The Race for Atomic Supremacy and Operation Paperclip's Contribution

Operation Paperclip: Unveiling the Covert U.S. Program that Recruited German Nazi Scientists

Historians and enthusiasts of Operation Paperclip: The Covert U.S. Program to Recruit German Nazi Scientists, get ready to uncover a fascinating chapter in history - The Race for Atomic Supremacy and Operation Paperclip's Contribution. This subchapter delves into the incredible impact that Operation Paperclip had on the United States' pursuit of atomic weaponry and the subsequent Cold War era.

As World War II came to a close, the United States found itself in a race against the Soviet Union for atomic supremacy. Recognizing the need for scientific expertise, Operation Paperclip was launched to recruit German Nazi scientists, many of whom possessed invaluable knowledge in nuclear physics and related fields. These brilliant minds, who were once instrumental in fueling Hitler's war machine, now found themselves at the forefront of America's atomic ambitions.

Under Operation Paperclip, German scientists such as Wernher von Braun, who played a pivotal role in the development of the V-2 rocket during the war, were brought to the United States. Their expertise and insights were harnessed by American scientists, propelling the nation's atomic research forward. The infusion of talent from Operation Paperclip undoubtedly gave the United States a significant advantage in the race for atomic supremacy.

The impact of Operation Paperclip on space exploration cannot be overstated. The German scientists recruited through this program played a crucial role in the formation of NASA and the development of the Saturn V rocket, which eventually propelled the Apollo missions to the moon. Without the contribution of these former Nazi scientists, America's space program would have faced substantial setbacks.

Furthermore, Operation Paperclip's influence on Cold War technology was profound. The knowledge and expertise of the German scientists enabled the United States to make significant advancements in missile technology, a critical component of the arms race with the Soviet Union. This covert program provided the U.S. military with a distinct advantage and contributed to the technological superiority that defined the Cold War era.

However, Operation Paperclip was not without ethical controversies and moral dilemmas. The decision to recruit former Nazi scientists raised questions about the United States' commitment to justice and accountability for war crimes. Critics argue that by providing immunity to these scientists, the U.S. compromised its moral standing.

Beyond the realms of space exploration and the arms race, Operation Paperclip's impact extended to various fields, including aeronautics, nuclear research, chemical warfare, intelligence, espionage, medical advancements, cybersecurity, and cryptography. This subchapter invites historians to explore the hidden yet influential legacy of Operation Paperclip in these diverse areas.

In conclusion, the Race for Atomic Supremacy and Operation Paperclip's Contribution is a captivating subchapter that sheds light on how the recruitment of German Nazi scientists under Operation Paperclip played a pivotal role in shaping America's pursuit of atomic weapons, space exploration, Cold War technology, and numerous other fields. It is a testament to the complex and multifaceted nature of this covert program and its enduring impact on history.

The Ethical Dilemmas of Employing Former Nazi Nuclear Scientists

Introduction:

Operation Paperclip, the covert U.S. program that recruited German Nazi scientists after World War II, remains a topic of intrigue and controversy. While the program undoubtedly contributed to significant advancements in various fields, it also raised profound ethical dilemmas. This subchapter explores the moral complexities surrounding the employment of former Nazi nuclear scientists and the lasting implications of their involvement.

Background:

Operation Paperclip aimed to harness the scientific expertise of German scientists, including those with ties to the Nazi regime, in order to gain an advantage during the emerging Cold War. Among these scientists were those specializing in nuclear research, a field of paramount importance in the post-war era. However, the decision to employ former Nazi nuclear scientists was not without its ethical challenges.

Ethical Dilemmas:

1. Complicity in War Crimes: Many of the scientists recruited under Operation Paperclip had active involvement in the Nazi regime and were complicit in war crimes. The employment of individuals connected

to such atrocities raises questions about moral responsibility and accountability.

2. Rehabilitation vs. Reward: By providing these scientists with prestigious positions and resources, Operation Paperclip essentially rewarded them for their expertise, potentially undermining the perception of justice and the rehabilitation of post-war Germany.

3. Ignoring Victims' Perspectives: The decision to employ former Nazi nuclear scientists disregarded the perspectives of Holocaust survivors and other victims who suffered directly or indirectly from the actions of these scientists. This raises concerns about prioritizing scientific advancement over justice and human rights.

4. Ethical Compromises in Research: The employment of former Nazi nuclear scientists may have led to compromises in ethical research practices. The desire for scientific progress and national security could have overshadowed concerns about experimentation on human subjects or the long-term consequences of nuclear technology.

Legacy and Implications:

The legacy of Operation Paperclip's employment of former Nazi nuclear scientists is multifaceted. On one hand, it played a crucial role in advancing nuclear research, leading to significant breakthroughs in energy production, medicine, and space exploration. On the other hand, it perpetuated a moral dilemma that continues to be debated today, with implications for the fields of aeronautics, intelligence, and cybersecurity.

Conclusion:

Operation Paperclip's employment of former Nazi nuclear scientists remains a highly contentious and morally complex aspect of history. It highlights the tension between scientific progress and ethical considerations, forcing us to grapple with the consequences of employing individuals involved in war crimes. Understanding the ethical dilemmas surrounding this program is crucial to contextualizing its impact on various fields and ensuring that we learn from the lessons of the past.

Chapter 10: Operation Paperclip: The Nazi Scientists' Involvement in Chemical Warfare

German Scientists' Expertise in Chemical Weapons Development

During World War II, German scientists played a crucial role in the development of chemical weapons for the Nazi regime. This subchapter explores the specific expertise of these scientists and their contributions to the field of chemical warfare. It sheds light on their involvement in Operation Paperclip, the covert U.S. program that recruited German Nazi scientists, and the impact it had on the subsequent development of chemical weapons.

Operation Paperclip aimed to capitalize on the scientific knowledge and technological advancements of German scientists, including those specializing in chemical warfare. These scientists possessed unparalleled expertise in the synthesis and deployment of deadly chemical agents, such as nerve agents like Sarin and VX.

Under the supervision of the U.S. military, these German scientists were brought to the United States to continue their research and development activities. Their knowledge and skills were harnessed to enhance America's own chemical weapons program, which was already underway during the war.

The German scientists' expertise greatly influenced the advancements made in chemical weapons technology during the Cold War era. Their contributions helped the United States gain a significant advantage in the arms race against the Soviet Union. The covert involvement of Operation Paperclip in the arms race remained undisclosed for many years, highlighting the secrecy surrounding the program.

Furthermore, the German scientists' involvement in chemical warfare had a lasting impact on medical advancements. Their research on chemical agents and their effects on the human body provided valuable insights into the development of antidotes and treatments for chemical weapon exposure.

However, the ethical controversies and moral dilemmas surrounding Operation Paperclip cannot be ignored. The program faced criticism for providing amnesty to Nazi scientists who had participated in war crimes and human experimentation. These scientists were given a fresh start in the United States, raising questions about the moral implications of their recruitment.

In conclusion, Operation Paperclip facilitated the recruitment of German scientists with expertise in chemical weapons development. Their contributions influenced the arms race, medical advancements, and the field of aeronautics. However, the program's ethical controversies and moral dilemmas remain a subject of debate among historians. Understanding the German scientists' influence on chemical warfare is crucial in comprehending the covert U.S. program and its long-lasting implications for various fields of research and technology.

Operation Paperclip's Impact on U.S. Chemical Warfare Capabilities

Operation Paperclip was a covert U.S. program that recruited German Nazi scientists after World War II. While its impact on various fields is well-documented, its influence on U.S. chemical warfare capabilities remains a lesser-known aspect. This subchapter aims to shed light on how Operation Paperclip shaped the development of chemical warfare in the United States.

Under Operation Paperclip, numerous German scientists with expertise in chemical warfare were brought to the U.S., despite their involvement in Nazi atrocities. They were given new identities, provided with employment, and granted immunity from prosecution in exchange for their knowledge and expertise. This influx of German scientists had a profound impact on U.S. chemical warfare capabilities, leading to advancements in both offensive and defensive measures.

The German scientists brought invaluable knowledge of chemical agents, including nerve gases and blistering agents, which were extensively tested and analyzed by the U.S. military. This knowledge significantly contributed to the development of more potent and effective chemical weapons. The U.S. chemical warfare program received a massive boost in terms of research and development, as these German scientists brought with them years of experience and expertise.

Moreover, Operation Paperclip played a crucial role in enhancing the U.S.'s defensive capabilities against chemical attacks. The German scientists' expertise helped develop improved gas masks, protective clothing, and decontamination techniques. Their knowledge of antidotes and medical treatments for chemical exposure also contributed to the development of effective countermeasures.

The impact of Operation Paperclip on U.S. chemical warfare capabilities extended beyond immediate military applications. The knowledge and research conducted by these scientists also had significant implications for civilian industries, such as pharmaceuticals and agriculture. The development of new pesticides, herbicides, and pharmaceutical drugs benefited greatly from the expertise brought by the German scientists.

However, the involvement of former Nazi scientists in the U.S. chemical warfare program raised ethical controversies and moral dilemmas. Critics argued that providing sanctuary and employment to these individuals undermined justice and accountability for their war crimes. The legacy of Operation Paperclip continues to be debated in terms of its ethical implications.

In conclusion, Operation Paperclip had a profound impact on U.S. chemical warfare capabilities. The recruitment of German Nazi scientists brought invaluable knowledge and expertise, leading to advancements in offensive and defensive measures. While the program contributed to the development of more potent chemical weapons, it also played a vital role in enhancing protective measures against chemical attacks. However, the ethical controversies surrounding the program cannot be ignored, as the legacy of Operation Paperclip continues to shape the field of chemical warfare and its moral implications.

The Legacy of German Scientists in the Field of Chemical Warfare

The subchapter titled "The Legacy of German Scientists in the Field of Chemical Warfare" delves into the significant contributions made by German scientists to the development of chemical warfare during and after World War II. This chapter explores the impact of Operation Paperclip, the covert U.S. program that recruited German Nazi scientists, on the advancement of chemical weapons research and technology.

Historians will find this subchapter particularly fascinating as it sheds light on the hidden involvement of German scientists in the development and refinement of chemical weapons, both during the war and in the post-war era. Operation Paperclip played a pivotal role in facilitating the transfer of knowledge and expertise from German scientists to the United States, ultimately shaping the trajectory of chemical warfare.

From the development of nerve agents like Tabun and Sarin to the enhancement of delivery systems and protective gear, German scientists brought their cutting-edge research to the American military-industrial complex. Their expertise significantly bolstered the United States' chemical warfare capabilities, ensuring that the country remained at the forefront of this deadly field.

Furthermore, this subchapter explores the ethical controversies and moral dilemmas associated with the recruitment of German Nazi scientists. It raises critical questions about the morality of employing individuals responsible for war crimes and human experimentation in the pursuit of military and scientific superiority. The legacy of Operation Paperclip in the field of chemical warfare forces us to confront the ethical implications of utilizing knowledge obtained through immoral means.

The subchapter also delves into the undisclosed impact of German scientists on cybersecurity and cryptography. With their deep understanding of encryption methods and code-breaking techniques, these scientists played a crucial role in advancing intelligence and espionage activities during the Cold War and beyond. Their expertise in chemical warfare extended beyond physical weapons, encompassing the manipulation of information and communication systems.

Overall, this subchapter provides historians with a comprehensive understanding of the legacy of German scientists in the field of chemical warfare. It highlights their significant contributions, ethical controversies, and hidden impacts on various niches such as intelligence, cybersecurity, and cryptography. By examining the hidden history of Operation Paperclip, this subchapter offers a unique perspective on the intricate connections between science, warfare, and the complex moral dilemmas that arise when scientific progress is intertwined with the atrocities of war.

The Ethical Implications of Utilizing Former Nazi Chemists

In the subchapter "The Ethical Implications of Utilizing Former Nazi Chemists," we delve into one of the most controversial aspects of Operation Paperclip, the covert U.S. program that recruited German Nazi scientists after World War II. This chapter aims to address historians and individuals interested in the various niches surrounding Operation Paperclip, including its impact on space exploration, Cold War technology, medical advancements, intelligence and espionage, aeronautics, nuclear research, chemical warfare, cybersecurity, and cryptography.

Operation Paperclip has long been shrouded in ethical controversies and moral dilemmas. The program sought to capitalize on the scientific knowledge and expertise possessed by former Nazi chemists, who had been involved in heinous war crimes and atrocities. The question arises: Is it ethically justifiable to utilize these scientists, knowing the atrocities they were associated with?

Critics argue that by employing these former Nazi chemists, the United States was effectively condoning their actions and undermining the principles of justice and accountability. Furthermore, it is argued that by granting them immunity from prosecution, Operation Paperclip sent a message that scientific knowledge and expertise outweighed the need for moral responsibility.

On the other hand, proponents of Operation Paperclip argue that the program was a necessary evil in order to gain a strategic advantage over the Soviet Union during the Cold War. By harnessing the knowledge of these scientists, the United States aimed to advance its own technological capabilities and prevent the Soviets from acquiring their expertise.

However, the ethical implications of Operation Paperclip go beyond the immediate aftermath of World War II. The legacy of these former Nazi chemists can be seen in the fields of aeronautics, space exploration, medical advancements, intelligence, and nuclear research. Their contributions, while significant, raise questions about the extent to which we should be willing to overlook past atrocities in the pursuit of scientific progress.

Ultimately, the subchapter on the ethical controversies and moral dilemmas surrounding Operation Paperclip aims to provoke thoughtful discussions among historians and individuals interested in the program's impact on various niches. The utilization of former Nazi chemists undoubtedly had far-reaching consequences, both positive and negative. Exploring these ethical implications serves as a reminder that the pursuit of scientific knowledge must always be accompanied by a deep understanding of the ethical responsibilities that come with it.

Chapter 11: Operation Paperclip: The Undisclosed Impact on Cybersecurity and Cryptography

German Scientists' Contributions to Cryptographic Systems

In the realm of cybersecurity and cryptography, German scientists have played a significant role in shaping the field, despite their controversial past as Nazi collaborators. This subchapter explores the contributions made by these scientists to cryptographic systems and the impact they had on the development of this critical aspect of modern technology.

Following World War II, the covert U.S. program known as Operation Paperclip recruited numerous German scientists, including those with expertise in cryptography. These scientists, who had previously worked on cryptographic systems for the Nazi regime, brought with them valuable knowledge and insights that would prove instrumental in advancing the field.

One of the most notable contributions came from Arthur Scherbius, the inventor of the Enigma machine, a device used by the Nazis to encrypt their communications during the war. Scherbius, along with other German scientists, provided invaluable information on the inner workings of the Enigma machine, helping the U.S. to decrypt intercepted Nazi messages. This breakthrough significantly aided the Allied war effort and is widely considered a turning point in the conflict.

Moreover, German scientists such as Max Newman and Tommy Flowers played a pivotal role in the development of the world's first programmable electronic computer, Colossus. This machine revolutionized codebreaking efforts by employing advanced parallel processing techniques, enabling the decryption of even more complex and sophisticated codes. The work of these German scientists laid the foundation for modern computer-based cryptographic systems and set the stage for the digital age.

Additionally, German scientists brought their expertise in mathematical and theoretical aspects of cryptography, making significant contributions to the field's theoretical foundations. Their research and insights into encryption algorithms, key distribution methods, and cryptanalysis techniques greatly advanced the understanding and practice of cryptography worldwide.

However, the involvement of these German scientists in Operation Paperclip raises ethical controversies and moral dilemmas. Many argue that by recruiting Nazi collaborators, the U.S. government condoned their actions and undermined the principles of justice and accountability. The legacy of Operation Paperclip is thus tarnished by these ethical concerns.

Nonetheless, the impact of German scientists on cryptographic systems cannot be understated. Their contributions laid the groundwork for modern cybersecurity and enabled the development of secure communication systems that are now integral to our daily lives. While their involvement in Operation Paperclip remains a contentious issue, the undeniable influence of these scientists on the field of cryptography cannot be overlooked.

Operation Paperclip's Influence on U.S. Intelligence Gathering

Operation Paperclip, the covert U.S. program that recruited German Nazi scientists, had a profound impact on U.S. intelligence gathering during and after World War II. This subchapter delves into the specific ways in which Operation Paperclip influenced the field of intelligence and espionage, shedding light on the significant contributions made by these scientists.

One of the key areas in which Operation Paperclip had a profound influence was in the development of advanced intelligence techniques. The Nazi scientists brought with them a wealth of knowledge and expertise in various fields, including cryptography, code-breaking, and signal intelligence. Their expertise and experience allowed the U.S. intelligence community to leapfrog ahead in the field of intelligence gathering, enabling them to intercept, decipher, and exploit enemy communications more effectively.

Another aspect where Operation Paperclip made a significant impact was in the development of cutting-edge surveillance technology. The German scientists possessed advanced knowledge in areas such as radar, sonar, and aerial reconnaissance, which greatly enhanced the U.S. ability to gather intelligence through covert means. Their expertise in these areas directly contributed to the development of sophisticated surveillance systems, enabling the U.S. to monitor enemy activities with unprecedented precision and accuracy.

Furthermore, Operation Paperclip played a crucial role in the establishment and expansion of U.S. intelligence agencies. The recruited scientists not only brought their technical expertise but also their strategic thinking and organizational skills. Their contributions helped shape the structure and operations of agencies such as the Central Intelligence Agency (CIA) and the National Security Agency (NSA), laying the foundation for the modern intelligence community in the United States.

Additionally, Operation Paperclip facilitated the exchange of intelligence between the U.S. and its allies. The Nazi scientists, having worked closely with German intelligence agencies, possessed valuable information on enemy tactics, technologies, and personnel. This information, when shared with U.S. intelligence agencies, greatly enhanced their ability to anticipate enemy actions and respond effectively.

However, it is important to acknowledge the ethical controversies and moral dilemmas surrounding Operation Paperclip. The decision to recruit former Nazi scientists, some of whom had been involved in war crimes, raised questions about the United States' commitment to justice and accountability. These ethical concerns continue to be debated among historians, forcing us to confront the complex nature of intelligence gathering and its inherent trade-offs.

In conclusion, Operation Paperclip had a far-reaching influence on U.S. intelligence gathering. The recruitment of German Nazi scientists brought invaluable expertise and knowledge to the field, revolutionizing intelligence techniques, surveillance technology, and the structure of intelligence agencies. However, the ethical controversies surrounding Operation Paperclip cannot be ignored, highlighting the delicate balance between national security and moral responsibility. Understanding the impact of Operation Paperclip is essential for historians and those interested in the intricate dynamics of intelligence and espionage.

The Legacy of German Scientists in Cybersecurity

In the realm of cybersecurity, the legacy of German scientists recruited through Operation Paperclip remains largely undisclosed and overlooked. However, their involvement in this field had a profound impact on the development of encryption techniques, cryptography, and the overall understanding of digital security.

One of the most notable contributions made by these German scientists was their expertise in cryptography. During World War II, German cryptographers had developed advanced encryption systems, such as the Enigma machine, which proved to be an immense challenge for the

Allied forces to crack. When these scientists were brought to the United States through Operation Paperclip, their knowledge and experience in cryptography became invaluable in the ongoing battle to secure sensitive information from potential adversaries.

Moreover, the German scientists played a crucial role in the development of early computer systems and their vulnerabilities. By studying the German cipher machines, they were able to identify weaknesses and subsequently devise countermeasures to enhance the security of American computer networks. Their work laid the foundation for modern cybersecurity practices, shaping the field as we know it today.

Furthermore, the German scientists' understanding of information warfare and psychological operations greatly influenced the American intelligence community. Drawing from their experiences in Nazi Germany, they provided invaluable insights into the potential threats posed by foreign intelligence agencies. Their expertise helped in the development of counterintelligence strategies that aimed to protect classified information from espionage and cyber-attacks.

Additionally, the German scientists' involvement in Operation Paperclip had a lasting impact on the ethical controversies and moral dilemmas surrounding the program. While their contributions to cybersecurity were significant, it is essential to acknowledge the questionable backgrounds of some of these scientists, who had previously been associated with the atrocities committed by the Nazi regime. The legacy of Operation Paperclip raises ethical questions about the extent to which the ends justified the means in recruiting these scientists.

In conclusion, the legacy of German scientists recruited through Operation Paperclip in the field of cybersecurity cannot be overstated. Their expertise in cryptography, computer systems, and intelligence played a pivotal role in shaping modern cybersecurity practices. However, their involvement also raises important ethical considerations that continue to be debated by historians and scholars alike. The untold story of their contribution to cybersecurity deserves further exploration and recognition.

The Ethical Considerations of Leveraging Former Nazi Expertise in the Digital Age

In the digital age, the world has become more interconnected than ever before. With advancements in technology and the rise of artificial intelligence, society has reaped numerous benefits. However, the question of ethics arises when considering the source of these advancements, particularly in the case of leveraging former Nazi expertise. Operation Paperclip, the covert U.S. program that recruited German Nazi scientists, has had a profound impact on various fields, including space exploration, cold war technology, medical advancements, intelligence and espionage, and even cybersecurity and cryptography.

For historians delving into the depths of Operation Paperclip, it is essential to evaluate the ethical controversies and moral dilemmas surrounding the utilization of Nazi expertise. The recruitment of these scientists, many of whom were complicit in war crimes, raises significant questions about accountability and justice. Should these individuals be given an opportunity to redeem themselves and contribute to society? Or does their involvement in the atrocities committed during World War II render them forever tainted?

Operation Paperclip's legacy in the field of aeronautics cannot be denied. The German scientists brought their knowledge and expertise, propelling the United States to new heights in aviation and rocketry. However, their involvement in nuclear research and chemical warfare also raises concerns about the potential misuse of their skills. Did the benefits outweigh the risks? And how do we navigate the delicate balance between progress and the potential for harm?

Moreover, Operation Paperclip's undisclosed impact on cybersecurity and cryptography is a matter of great significance in the digital age. The knowledge and expertise these scientists possessed undoubtedly contributed to advancements in these fields. Yet, the very act of employing individuals with questionable ethics raises concerns about the integrity and trustworthiness of the technology they helped develop. Can we truly rely on systems and algorithms built upon a foundation tainted by Nazi collaboration?

As historians explore the intricate details of Operation Paperclip, it is crucial to address the ethical controversies and moral dilemmas that arise. The legacy of this covert program extends far beyond its immediate impact, shaping fields such as space exploration, cold war technology, and medical advancements. However, we must critically examine the source of these advancements and consider the potential consequences of leveraging former Nazi expertise in the digital age. Only by doing so can we navigate the delicate balance between progress and the ethical considerations that shape our society.